God, My Creator

The Apostles' Creed

Jim Gimbel and Jo Gimbel
Illustrated by Susan Morris

Explanation of the First Article of the Apostles' Creed taken from
Luther's Small Catechism with Explanation © 1986 Concordia Publishing House.

Arch® Books
Copyright © 2003 Concordia Publishing House
3558 S. Jefferson Avenue, St. Louis, MO 63118-3968
Manufactured in Colombia

The apostle quit speaking; the crowd went away.
But 8-year-old Michael decided to stay.
He had lots of questions; his face was aglow.
This God-of-Three-Persons he wanted to know.

So Michael ran up to Bartholomew's side.
"Please teach me, I want to know more," the boy cried.
Bartholomew had a kind look on his face.
His smile and manner reflected God's grace.

"What can we say to show God's for real?
We can't see Him or hear Him—His hand we can't feel!
I believe," the boy said, "I'm baptized; I'm His own.
But how is it then that this God becomes known?"

Bartholomew thought for a minute, then said,
"You're wise, my young friend, to think with your head.
True believing involves both the head and the heart.
Also, loving and living set this faith apart."

Then Michael looked 'round and saw other gods too.
He asked, "Why do we say that just our God is true?"
Bartholomew gave a loud chuckle, "You see,
He's different and better than any of these!

"Those gods are just statues; they're not kind or good.
Their image is carved out of marble or wood.
They're not living or real; they can't help in our need.
They can't listen, no matter how long we might plead."

"Let's talk first of knowing the God we can't see.
His fingerprints mark every bush, every tree.
Each animal, too, whether big or quite small—
By the Word of His mouth, God created them all.

"He made Earth out of nothing. He spoke; it was so.
He made raindrops and hail and fluffy, white snow.
He made sun, moon, and stars that give off their light.
He keeps nature in balance, things that fall—things in flight."

"Then last, but not least, God made the first man
To work and take care of it all was His plan.
God made brains that could think and eyes that could see;
He made every small part that together makes 'me.'

"He made us complete, with both body and soul
So we'd live with Him always 'cause that was His goal.
He also made angels to do what He says.
Every bit of creation's most certainly His!"

"Of millions of people no two are alike,
Each person is special like you, my dear Mike.
God gives families who love us, our moms and dads too,
Helped by teachers and leaders who guide our way through.

"God gives people homes; He provides them with clothes.
He gives fish, fruit, and vegetables, even bread loaves.
He gives all that we have; He gives all that we need.
He protects, He defends, and He truly will lead.

"But as great as He is with His power and all,
He loves us enough to hear when we call.
He's the best Father ever; He's firm and He's fair.
There's nothing so strong as His great, tender care."

"Though all was made perfect in only six days,
The first people did evil and went their own ways.
But our Father is loving and sent His own Son.
Through Jesus, the Savior, forgiveness was won.

"He wants us to trust Him with all of our heart
But even this act is His gift from the start.
He helps us be thankful and sing to His praise,
To serve and obey Him for all of our days."

Michael believed; his faith and trust grew.
The love of his heavenly Father was true.
When he went home that night, he had peace and true joy
Because he knew God the Father loved His little boy.

Martin Luther's Meaning to the First Article

What does this mean?

I believe that God has made me and all creatures; that He has given me my body and soul, eyes, ears, and all my members, my reason and all my senses, and still takes care of them.

He also gives me clothing and shoes, food and drink, house and home, wife and children, land, animals, and all I have. He richly and daily provides me with all that I need to support this body and life.

He defends me against all danger and guards and protects me from all evil.

All this He does only out of fatherly, divine goodness and mercy, without any merit or worthiness in me. For this it is my duty to thank and praise, serve and obey Him.

This is most certainly true.

I believe in God, the Father Almighty,
Maker of heaven and earth.

And in Jesus Christ, His only Son, our Lord,
who was conceived by the Holy Spirit,
born of the Virgin Mary,
suffered under Pontius Pilate,
was crucified, died and was buried.
He descended into hell.
the third day He rose again from the dead.
He ascended into heaven
   and sits at the right hand of God,
   the Father Almighty.
From thence He will come to judge
the living and the dead.

I believe in the Holy Spirit,
the holy Christian church,
the communion of saints,
the forgiveness of sins,
the resurrection of the body,
and the life everlasting. Amen.

The Apostles' Creed

Dear parents,

Your child is just learning many of the truths the Bible teaches about God, especially how He can be three persons and still be only one God. This concept is beyond what even we as adults can fully understand, but we accept it in faith—the faith God creates in both children and adults through His almighty Word and the gift of Holy Baptism.

When we say the words of the First Article of the Apostles' Creed, we are expressing together, with all those who believe in Him, what the Bible teaches about the First Person of the Trinity. The Bible describes how God created the whole world and set the laws of nature in place to keep it functional and still takes care of it. The Bible also teaches that God took special care when He made people, breathing into them the breath of life and promising to preserve their lives. After sin ruined God's perfect world, God gave people a second chance to live with Him through faith in His Son, Jesus. There is no greater treasure for your child to possess than a living faith, which confesses the words of the creed, saying, "I believe."

Help your child learn the words of the creed and encourage him or her to say them with you in worship and at home. Help your child see God's hand in nature when you are enjoying His creation. Talk about ways He continues to care for it and for you. Then pray or sing together the words of the doxology:

"Praise God, from whom all blessings flow;
Praise Him, all creatures here below;
Praise Him above, ye heav'nly host;
Praise Father, Son, and Holy Ghost."

The Authors